NOTE TO SELF

CHAPTER

II

WRITTEN BY

CHIDOZIE E. OSUWA

outskirts
press

Outskirts Press, Inc.
http://www.outskirtspress.com

ISBN: 978-1-9772-1603-8

<u>Note to self:</u>
Sweetheart, you weren't put on this earth to be someone's second choice 6:53 PM.

Don't wait around for someone to come back after it doesn't work with the person they chose over you. You're nobody's safety net.

<u>Note to self:</u>
Fix yourself before you go pursuing people and pulling them into your chaos.
12:19 AM.

We need to stop trying to use others to heal ourselves. It is not fair to them. Stop pulling people into your hurt and pain. Become whole again, before you go looking for love.

<u>Note to self:</u>
Forgetting someone ever existed is better than holding a grudge.
3:23 PM.

Holding a grudge only hinders your own happiness. Let it go. Let them go. Live your life.

<u>Note to self:</u>
Never let someone make you feel like your feelings are invalid. They matter. You matter.
4:56 AM.

You deserve someone who will listen to your concerns and work to fix them. Don't suffer in silence.

Note to self:
You don't need people in your life that don't have a role or a purpose.
6:34 PM.

Surround yourself with people who celebrate you and genuinely want to be a part of your life. Stay away from people who do the minimum to maintain access to you just for their own benefit.

Note to self:
**Someone who values you will not play games with your feelings or time, because they don't want to put themselves in the position to lose you.
11:33 AM.**

<u>Note to self:</u>
You deserve a man who is going to add to your life, and build you up. Not someone who just expects you to hold him down through everything he puts you through.
6:53 PM.

Too often we hear about men saying they want a "ride or die chick". What I find funny is that we almost never hear these same men talking about being a "ride or die man" for their woman.

<u>Note to self:</u>
People will use you, move on to the next, and feel nothing. Be careful.
10:02 AM.

Never underestimate how selfish people are. Be careful giving people too much too soon. Learn their character, first, and move accordingly.

<u>Note to self:</u>
You can't change a man. He'll change when he wants to. And if he doesn't change for you, then you may just have to accept that you weren't the one.
9:55 AM.

One of the tough realities to accept is that the person we wanted to be "the one" simply is not. A lot of times, we want what we want with who we want so bad that we try to hold on far longer than we know we should. I pray you learn to accept that certain people are not for you no matter how bad you wish they are.

<u>Note to self:</u>
Go ahead and start over. It won't kill you. It just might save you.
4:55 PM.

We have to learn that starting over is not the worst thing in the world. In some cases, it just may be the best and most liberating thing you can do for yourself. Yes, it can be scary, but it can also be what saves you.

<u>Note to self:</u>
Make sure they can't come back after finding out that the grass wasn't greener. 3:21 PM.

Be unavailable. Don't wait around for someone to choose you. Never let someone feel like they can leave and come back whenever they feel like they are missing out on something.

<u>Note to self:</u>
You deserve forehead kisses
and butt rubs from a man
who chooses you daily.
9:12 PM.

<u>Note to self:</u>
Even as strong as you are, you're allowed to be tired of someone's bullshit.
4:12 PM.

Being strong is not always about enduring everything thrown your way. Sometimes, the greatest display of strength is your ability to walk away.

Note to self:

Maybe you need to consider that you do too much for people who do nothing for you.
6:14 PM.

Make sure that person you are giving 100 percent of you is also giving you 100 percent of them. You should not be fully committed and pouring into someone who always seems to have one foot in and one foot out.

<u>Note to self:</u>
If he stopped trying after he got you, it's because he never really valued you in the first place. He only wanted you. That's it.
7:42 AM

It's not hard to find a man who wants you. The key is finding one who values you. A man who wants you can pretend for a while, but eventually, his effort and consistency fades when he feels he has you. A man who values you will do what it takes to get you, and continue to do what it takes to keep you.

<u>Note to self:</u>
Don't let him hide you. You are a prize. And you deserve someone who is proud of you.
4:52 PM.

There is a difference between keeping your relationship private, and hiding your partner, or the fact that you are in a relationship to begin with.

<u>Note to self:</u>
Fuck that "one last conversation" you think you need to have with him. You've had too many of those, already. Nothing changed. It'll just be an opportunity for him to feed you more bullshit and pull you back in.
2:48 AM.

<u>Note to self:</u>
Worry less about how you both look together, and more about how it feels to be with them.
8:42 PM.

Too many people are more worried about being able to take cute pictures than they are with building a healthy and loving relationship with their partner. It's not about how it looks to the public, It's about how it feels to you and yours.

<u>Note to self:</u>
**May you have the strength to wait for what you know you want and need. It's hard but it's worth it.
6:16 AM.**

<u>Note to self:</u>
There is a man out there who wants to spoil you with time, effort, and consistency. Don't settle. 9:21 AM.

Don't let society convince you that the kind of love you yearn for does not exist. It does. And you deserve every bit of it.

<u>Note to self:</u>
Don't ever lower your standards to keep someone. They need to be growing with you.
5:14 PM.

Lowering your standards for someone is a disservice to yourself. You should not have to settle for less than. Any one who cannot rise up to meet your standards is simply not the one for you.

<u>Note to self:</u>

You deserve someone you don't have to keep an eye on 24/7. You should be able to trust your partner without them making you regret it. 1:12 AM.

Relationships can't work without trust. If it scares you to be away from your partner because you are not sure what they may do in your absence, then perhaps you are with the wrong person.

<u>Note to self:</u>
Don't be the woman bragging on social media about a relationship that you are miserable in.
9:33 AM.

Too many people stay in toxic relationships because they are trying to "prove the haters wrong". The only person that loses when you are unhappy in real life is you.

<u>Note to self:</u>
When you're a priority to him, you'll know. Until then, act accordingly.
2:52 PM.

Stop rearranging your life for someone who hasn't even made you a priority in theirs. Know the situation you are in, and play it accordingly. Prioritize people as they prioritize you.

Note to self:
**Stop pretending that you don't see the signs.
1:20 PM.**

<u>Note to self:</u>
Make sure that you are falling in Love because you are ready, and not just accepting whatever comes because you are lonely. 2:11 AM.

Loneliness can cause you to settle. We all want someone. But settling for anything just to have someone next to you is not it. Don't cheat yourself. If you're always settling because you don't like being alone, you will never get what it is you know that you deserve.

Note to self:

Learn to exit people's lives quietly, without a fuss. Let them find out that they no longer have access to you when they try to get in contact.
5:33 PM.

<u>Note to self:</u>
You deserve a man that you don't have to give 174 chances because he gets it the first or second time. 3:36 PM.

<u>Note to self:</u>
**Imagine someone who communicates their feelings, and thoughts, and doesn't keep you in the dark, guessing.
6:19 AM.**

You shouldn't be in any relationship that leaves you unsure about how he feels, and where you stand with your partner. There should always be communication and transparency.

<u>Note to self:</u>
Be mature enough to know when to work things out, smart enough to know when to leave, and strong enough to actually leave.
7:35 AM.

Some problems are fixable. It's not about leaving every time your partner does something you don't like. It's about patterns and the overall feeling and atmosphere of the relationship. You deserve effort, respect, consistency, and a love you don't have to question. But even with all those things, there will be arguments, and quarrels, as you are different people. It's all about the person's willingness to resolve those issues, and or address your concerns. It's about making sure they aren't deliberately disrespecting you, and taking you for granted. It's about making sure they value you, and it shows.

Note to self:

You deserve a man who maintains the same effort and energy he had when he was still trying to "win" you. 5:47 PM.

A man should not stop trying once he "gets you". That was only the beginning. It's like going on an interview, getting the job, and then coming in and doing nothing once you are hired. You'll most likely be fired.

<u>Note to self:</u>
Never beg a man for things you know you deserve.
2:47 AM.

Any man who approaches you without already knowing your value and worth, is a man you shouldn't waste your time with.

<u>Note to self:</u>
Stop taking people back who haven't fixed anything about themselves.
7:15 PM.

This is one of the most effective ways to get yourself hurt or disappointed again. I know you wished it worked out. I know you may even still want it to work, now. But if they were the problem, and nothing about them has been fixed or changed, you are surely going to get the same result.

<u>Note to self:</u>
Allow them to lose you before you lose yourself. 5:32 AM.

Sometimes, you have to save yourself from the person you want. Sometimes, "losing" them is the blessing.

<u>Note to self:</u>
Go on that date. Your ex isn't coming back. He hasn't changed. It's time to move on.

9:52 AM.

Stop waiting for who you are supposed to be leaving behind to reach out to you and find it's way back into your life. Decide that you want to move on, and move on!

<u>Note to self:</u>

**Hold on to the people who show you that they want to be a part of your life.
9:16 PM.**

The people who don't make the effort to be a part of your life do not deserve to be. Stop allowing inconsistent and convenient relationships take up space and time in your life.

<u>Note to self:</u>
**Make sure you are as important to them as you think you are.
2:11 AM.**

Make sure the way you view them is the way they view you. Make sure the way you think they feel about you, is the way they actually do. Have conversations with them about you, and about the relationship, and observe their actions.

<u>Note to self:</u>
Being loyal does not mean being his dummy.
6:39 AM.

Loyalty does not mean you need to become the woman he can walk all over, use, cheat on, and come back to. That's not loyalty. That is abuse.

<u>Note to self:</u>
No amount of loyalty you give the wrong man is going to turn him into the right one.
3:48 PM.

You cannot love someone into treating you right. You will only drain yourself and end up walking away as a shell of who you once were.

<u>Note to self:</u>
Don't give up on love. But definitely feel free to give up on that man who is not trying. You're allowed to. You deserve effort. 8:27 AM.

Never let the people who were incapable of loving you correctly cause you to give up on love. Love isn't the problem; they are.

<u>Note to self:</u>
Laughter, happiness
and peace should come
standard with whomever
you choose to date. Life is
too short for anything else.
2:37 AM.

<u>Note to self:</u>
Be willing to wait for better, instead of jumping at every half ass man who shows interest.
7:22 PM.

As long as you are always willing to accept whatever it is someone offers you, you will never get what you are worth, and deserve.

<u>Note to self:</u>
You deserve a man that hypes you up daily.
4:55 AM.

You deserve a man who is not only your best friend, but also your loudest cheerleader! You deserve someone who simply loves to see you be you!

<u>Note to self:</u>
Dating should be fun. If it's draining, then that's a sign that that person may not be a good fit for you.
7:09 AM.

Your relationship should be what fills you up, not what drains you. You should be excited about each other. Anyone who makes this difficult is someone you should stop giving your time to.

<u>Note to self:</u>
Don't let good sex take precedence over how he treats you.
9:22 AM.

Too often women echo this false notion that good sex typically comes from toxic men. I believe this is false. I believe that good sex can be found in all kinds of men, INCLUDING toxic men. And just because that's where you have been finding it because of the kind of men you have been dating, does not mean that is the only place it exists. Secondly, that should never be more important than the way a man treats you. EVER.

<u>Note to self:</u>
How he treats you tells you two things - How he feels about you, and how he feels about himself. Pay attention. 12:22 PM.

Don't convince yourself that someone feels for you more than they have shown you just because of what you feel for them. Feelings aren't automatically reciprocated.

<u>Note to self:</u>
You deserve someone who chooses you over and over again, every single day; Without question; without hesitation.
3:52 AM.

<u>Note to self:</u>
Let him miss you for a while. You have been way too available and accessible. 1:01 AM.

Sometimes, a man can begin to take you for granted when you are always there at his convenience even with his inconsistency. If he's consistent and prioritizes you, then that's one thing. But you don't need to be "on call" for people who are inconsistent, and only hit you up when they either want something from you, or their other "options" are too busy for them.

<u>Note to self:</u>
If he's not making his intentions clear, keep your options open. You don't need to commit to people who do not commit to you. 3:53 AM.

Any 'man' who isn't man enough to claim you and let you know his intentions with you, is not someone you need to be betting your future on.

Note to self:
As a woman, your attitude should be 'fuck any man you have to chase'.
4:08 AM.

<u>Note to self:</u>
Fuck what you feel. Always remember what you deserve.
9:51 AM.

Don't let how much you like someone cause you to be out here tolerating any kind of treatment. What you deserve should always be top priority.

<u>Note to self:</u>
People reach out when they notice you moving on. Stay woke.
5:02 AM.

Don't let any toxic person from your past drag you back into their bullshit when you are on the verge of moving on, when you've moved on, or when you are trying to move on, PERIOD!

Note to self:
Cry if you have to, and then let that shit go.
12:22 PM.

<u>Note to self:</u>
When a man really wants you, you won't be confused about it.
7:27 PM.

If he's sending you mixed signals, it's because he's unsure or doesn't want you. Take that as a sign, and walk away, because any man who is unsure is surely about to waste your time.

<u>Note to self:</u>
Stop getting comfortable with accepting half effort, and inconsistent love.
6:12 AM.

If you want people to be consistent, then you have to learn to stop accepting inconsistency. If they keep getting away with only getting back to you when they feel like it or being able to get all of you just by giving the minimum, then they will continue to do so.

<u>Note to self:</u>
You know how you know someone is lying but you kind of force yourself to believe it because you really like them…? Yeah, stop that shit.
4:09 PM.

Purposely being naïve to a truth that is right in front of you will not alter the reality of what is going on. You have to face it and either avoid wasting time, or hurting yourself further down the line.

<u>Note to self:</u>
Remember this – being loyal to the wrong person will have you looking like a complete fool.
5:32 AM.

Too many women stay in failing relationships because they are trying to "prove how loyal they are". Please do not be one. Know when to leave. You gain nothing by "proving" this at the cost of your own happiness.

<u>Note to self:</u>
You're not obligated to do wifey things for a man who is not doing husband things for you.
4:32 AM.

Stop letting these men convince you that you are obligated to doing things for them that they themselves don't reciprocate in the relationship. There are levels to a relationship. Make people earn parts of you as they grow with you.

<u>Note to self:</u>
Stop wasting your time with people who are not showing much interest in you.
2:44 AM.

It's about who you like, but don't forget, it's also about who likes you back.

<u>Note to self:</u>
Learn the difference between being in love, and being comfortable with what you know.
5:33 AM.

A lot of times, people aren't really in love. They are just comfortable. Comfortable with who they know... comfortable with the routine that involves that person.

<u>Note to self:</u>
You won't have to convince a real man of your worth. He'll see it before he even approaches you. 7:13 AM.

<u>Note to self:</u>
Don't let him steal you joy and go smile in the next chick's face. Don't let him win like that.
3:19 PM.

Consider this - the man that you are sitting in the house crying over is probably out living his best life. Stop letting that hurt control you. Stop letting it consume you.

<u>Note to self:</u>
When they come back after they find out that the person they switched up on you for isn't shit, make sure you're inaccessible.
4:09 AM.

Don't be the woman he can run back to after choosing everyone else before you.

Note to self:
One of the best feelings in the world is realizing you are truly done with a toxic person. I mean to the point you are no longer affected by what they do.
10:02 AM.

<u>Note to self:</u>
Sometimes you have to protect yourself... even from someone you love.
6:51 AM.

At some point in life, you'll have to learn how to love people from a distance. This doesn't only apply to relationships. This applies to friends and family, as well.

<u>Note to self:</u>
**Stop accepting mediocre treatment just to have someone there.
5:23 AM.**

<u>Note to self:</u>
Stop giving people from your past the power to ruin your present.
6:12 AM.

When you leave people in your past, make sure you really leave them there. Don't look back, don't reach out to them, don't watch them, and don't invest any more of yourself in them or their actions. Be truly free.

<u>Note to self:</u>
Stop exchanging all of you for half of them.
4:33 PM.

Make sure your effort is reciprocated. Make sure you are receiving a fair exchange of energy and effort from people you are pouring into.

<u>Note to self:</u>
**Real love is rare. Hold on to it.
3:12 AM.**

Note to self:
Get out of your feelings. He's already with the next chick.
6:15 PM.

Stop waiting around. Stop being angry. Stop wondering "what if he calls", and decide to move on. The sooner you make the decision to be done with it, the sooner your healing process can begin, and you can actually move past it.

<u>Note to self:</u>
You're not hard to love. A lot of men just pretend they are ready until they realize you are serious.
2:02 AM.

A lot of times, men like the idea of having a particular woman, until they start to see what all it takes to get and keep her. Especially men who may be used to women who let them come and go as they please and do what they want. When they run into a real woman who requires real effort, and real consistency, they have no idea what to do, so they attempt to blame shift.

<u>Note to self:</u>
You deserve to experience a
healthy relationship.
We all do.
4:56 PM.

Note to self:
**Evolve into a woman your exes can't even recognize or reach.
7:17 AM.**

Note to self:
**Stop dealing with people who never own their faults. They will never change because they can't even admit that change is needed.
1:19 AM.**

<u>Note to self</u>:
Stop dealing with men who think you are trying to start an argument every time you express your feelings. They still have some growing to do.
3:34 PM.

<u>Note to self:</u>
Allowing him to disrespect you won't make him love you more or better.
2:21 AM.

Don't ever subscribe to the notion that letting a man put you through hell is the way to receive the kind of love that you deserve. That whole "ride or die" ideology is very juvenile. Be with the man who is willing to go through hell with you, not one who is ok with putting you through it.

Note to self:

Don't convince yourself that it's not as bad as you know it is. Don't convince yourself that lying and cheating is ok, or normal. Don't convince yourself that constant misery and pain are a part of love.
5:19 AM.

<u>Note to self:</u>
Don't be the woman who knows her worth but has gotten too comfortable in a shitty relationship with an unworthy man.
8:12 AM.

<u>Note to self:</u>
The man you are praying for is also praying for you.
2:55 AM.

The kind of love that you seek will find you. When it does, I pray that you are ready to let it in.

<u>Note to self:</u>
You deserve the kind of man you brag to your friends about… about the way he loves you… about the way he treats you… consistently. 5:12 AM.

<u>Note to self:</u>
You deserve a man who's willing to listen to your concerns, and address them. Not one who minimizes your feelings. 8:44 PM.

Stop dealing with men who make you feel guilty for having feelings, and voicing them. Your partner should want to hear those feelings and thoughts. He should want to know what he can do better to keep you happy, and vice versa.

<u>Note to self:</u>
**Consistency, respect, and faithfulness are the basics. Don't let this new generation of lazy lovers convince you otherwise.
5:11 PM.**

Note to self:
A man who truly cares about you will distance himself from things that threaten the relationship.
2:21 AM.

Don't let any man continuously feed you excuses as to why he cannot stop putting himself in situations that make you uncomfortable. That is a man who doesn't truly care about your feelings and concerns. A man who values the relationship will do everything in his power to make sure his woman feels secure and reassured.

<u>Note to self:</u>
Start doing what's best for you. They have already been doing what's best for them. 3:13 AM

<u>Note to self:</u>
A real man wont embarrass you, because he understands that embarrassing you is also embarrassing himself.
8:14 AM.

A real man in a relationship understands that not only does he represent himself, or you, as individuals, but he also represents the relationship as a whole; he represents the both of you as a team. He also understands that embarrassing you is an embarrassment to who he is as a man, as it speaks to his character.

Note to self:

Don't let any man feed you just enough false hope to maintain access to you for his own benefit.
4:13 PM.

Men are very good at playing into your feelings and emotions. They know what to say to string you along. Make sure he is not taking advantage of what he knows you are hoping for and keeping you around with no intention on coming through on any promises.

<u>Note to self:</u>
Stop putting up with toxic people because of who they used to be... or who they pretended to be.
2:12 PM.

Accept that people may change, or simply show their true self, in time. Too often we hold on to how things were in the "honeymoon phase" of a relationship, hoping that someday, things will go back to that. Sometimes, you just have to consider that may, that was not who they truly were.

<u>Note to self:</u>
Learn to be loyal to yourself, first. And leave things alone that are a betrayal to your self-love.
7:13 PM.

When you start to really love yourself, some of the things that you used to put up with won't even be able to make their way into your space. You have to love yourself to the point where people are afraid to approach you with bullshit.

<u>**Note to self:**</u>
Don't waste your time with men who say they aren't ready. It's not your job to convince them to be. A man who truly wants you will get himself ready before he even tries to become a part of your life.
4:12 PM.

<u>Note to self:</u>
Stop hurting in silence.
3:12 PM.

Tell the person how you feel, so they can have a chance on resolving it. So that they can decide if they want to fix it or not, and you can decide if you want to move forward or move on.

<u>Note to self:</u>
The reason he keeps doing the same things he just apologized for is because you have shown him too many times that he can get away with it.
3:12 PM.

<u>Note to self:</u>

I'm at a point in my life where I don't want to waste anyone's time because that would include wasting my own time.
9:12 PM.

This comes with growth. This comes with realizing that your time is too valuable to spend playing games with people. Unfortunately, not everyone is wise enough to understand this.

<u>Note to self:</u>
Stay away from people who will say you are hard to love because you expect effort and consistency. They aren't qualified to love you.
7:34 AM.

Honestly, these are things you shouldn't even have to ask for. If you do, then that should be your first sign right there, that, maybe, that person is not serious about you.

<u>Note to self:</u>
Be your own peace.
7:44 PM.

It's no one's job to bring you peace.
You need to be at peace with yourself.
Anyone else should only add to that.
Stop expecting people to create your
own peace and joy when you haven't
been able to find that within yourself.

<u>Note to self:</u>
The goal is someone who matches your energy, effort, and grind. Lets grow together.
9:15 PM.

Honestly, anything less is cheating yourself.

<u>Note to self:</u>
They'll beg for your attention and time, and then fumble it.
5:37 PM.

Take the hint. If someone doesn't value your time, do not keep giving it to them. At that point, you are the one wasting your own time. Learn your lesson, and keep it moving.

<u>Note to self:</u>
Forgiving them is for your own peace of mind. Not inviting them back into your life is also for your own peace of mind.
7:12 PM.

All forgiveness does not have to come with access back into your life. Know the people you need to keep at a distance, and the people you can allow back into your space.

<u>Note to self:</u>
Leave his ass right where he had you "fucked up" at. 12:12 PM.

There are some things that a person can do that they just don't get to recover from. Some disrespect is just too much to overlook.

<u>Note to self:</u>
Being a good person is hard. But, please, don't let the world change you. 3:37 PM.

It's hard to continue to be a good and kind person, especially when you feel like people keep on taking you for granted. But don't let that change who you are. You will win in the end. Good things find good people.

<u>Note to self:</u>
Once I get used to not talking to you, you are fucked.
8:51 AM.

The moment you are able to break the routine that involves them, the easier moving on becomes, and the more difficult it becomes for them to insert themselves back into your life.

<u>Note to self:</u>
**You are beautiful even when broken. You are worthy, even after all you've been through.
5:37 AM.**

Stop questioning if you're worth it. You are. Those who were unable to see your worth didn't change your value. Those experiences have made you better, not worse. That pain has made you stronger, not weaker. You are better now than you ever were.

<u>Note to self:</u>
It's ok to miss someone even after you realize that they are no good for you; it happens; you're human. But, please find the courage to stay away.
6:44 PM.

No, there is nothing wrong with you because you miss someone who was toxic to you. A lot of times, what you miss more so is the routine you developed with that person. That's normal. But please understand that is not a sign that you need to go back or let that person back into your space.

<u>Note to self:</u>
Choose single and at peace over fake love.
7:03 PM.

Fake love will never fulfill you. Having just anyone around will not give you that feeling that you truly yearn for. Wait for something real. Wait for something worth it.

<u>Note to self:</u>
Prepare for what you prayed for… because it's coming. 3:04 PM.

You have to believe that better is out there, and going to find you. That is what makes those nights alone worth it. And that's the energy that will attract that kind of love that you want.

Note to self:
Sex is truly amazing when you're in love.
6:23 PM.

<u>Note to self:</u>
That pain won't last forever, I promise. Keep going. 5:04 PM.

Time will help heal you. Notice I said "HELP". Meaning you, yourself, also have a part to play. You have to decide that you actually want to heal. You have to decide that you actually want to move on, and start the process for yourself. This means stop looking back, and wondering "what if?"

<u>Note to self:</u>
Loyalty is a choice; not some impossible task like some people try to make it seem.
3:06 PM.

Don't let anyone convince you that it is impossible for a man to be faithful to one woman. It is very possible. Men who say this just want to make excuses for themselves in advance so that they can have the leeway to cheat.

<u>Note to self:</u>
Sis, stop trying to date his potential.
6:39 AM.

<u>Note to self:</u>
Do not hate people. Just leave them alone.
8:49 PM.

I heard once that the opposite of Love is not hate, as many believe; but that the opposite of love is indifference. To be completely and utterly unaffected by someone, one way or another; because hate requires energy... which only shows that you still care. So let that grudge go. Invest no more feelings into that person, and go live your life.

<u>Note to self:</u>
**Nothing worse than a man whose woman has to teach him how to be a man.
3:19 AM.**

You're not his mother. While there is nothing wrong with showing your man new things, and teaching him your love language and such, you should not have to feel like you are raising a grown up.

<u>Note to self:</u>
Date yourself for a while.
Treat yourself like you
deserve.
11:05 AM.

Don't just spend your time being single
waiting for someone to find you and
treat you how you want to be treated.
You have to set the bar of how you want
others to treat you by the way you treat
yourself. Create that example before
anyone ever even approaches you.

<u>Note to self:</u>
Stop loving men in public who only love you in private. Claim who claims you. 5:09 PM.

Make sure the person you are celebrating is celebrating you as well. Everything must be mutual. You should be with someone who is proud of you, and shows you through his actions. Now, I'm not saying you should be so focused on whether your partner is posting you on social media, however, I am saying that you should not feel like you are being hidden or kept a secret.

<u>Note to self:</u>
Be with someone who doesn't want to go days without talking to you.
6:12 AM.

Even when your partner is mad at you, I pray that the love and connection that they have for you always outweighs that. I pray you choose a partner who wants to resolve issues with you as soon as possible so that they can get right back to celebrating you.

<u>Note to self:</u>
Never try to hold on to a man who already has his hands on the next woman. 7:55 PM.

We have to learn to stop chasing or waiting for people who have already moved on. No matter how much you wished it worked, or still hope that it can, learn to accept what is. The fact that they were able to move on that fast, or without fighting for you, should speak to how much they don't or didn't really care for the relationship. Let that be all the motivation you need to let go and move on.

<u>Note to self:</u>
There's something particularly sexy about someone who's only focused on you.
12:01 PM.

We all deserve that feeling of absolute security in our relationship. The feeling of absolute trust in knowing that your partner cherishes you and only you.
No one deserves to be in a relationship where they constantly have to wonder if they are enough, or feel like they are still in competition with others for the attention and love of the person they are with.

<u>Note to self:</u>
This next version of you emerging is going to be epic. Keep growing. 6:09 PM.

Never stop growing. Never stop elevating, even after love finds you. Be with someone who can grow with you. Be with someone who pushes you to be the best version of yourself.

<u>Note to self:</u>
The same people who will abuse and misuse you will tell you that you've changed.
8:34 PM.

The nerve of any man who damages a woman to then turn around and blame her for not being who she once was. The nerve of a man to fault a woman because he is unable to handle the person that he has turned her into.

<u>Note to self:</u>
You don't need them to validate you. You are the shit. You've been that before anyone, and you'll be that after anyone. Own it.
5:39 PM.

When you realize your worth, you stop seeking validation from anyone else because you give it to yourself. You find yourself being a lot happier because that happiness is no longer controlled by others.

<u>Note to self:</u>
Don't chase after anyone to prove to them that you matter.
6:06 PM.

Make room in your life for the people who willingly want to stay. The people who want to celebrate you, not the people who merely tolerate you. Being a part of your life is a privilege. Knowing you is a privilege. Having access to you is a privilege. Act accordingly.

<u>Note to self:</u>
Dating in this era is tough. Everyone is entitled, never wrong, and "doesn't give a fuck".
4:19 AM

I pray you find someone who isn't afraid to show that they care. In fact, I pray you find someone who wants to show that they care. Someone who is understanding, and ok with admitting their faults. This whole "I don't give a fuck" attitude that so many adults of our generation have adopted isn't healthy, especially in relationships. You should care... for the people who care about you. And you shouldn't be afraid to show it.

<u>Note to self:</u>
Starting today, stop reaching out to people who haven't been reaching back. 5:02 AM

If you are always the one reaching out to someone, you may need to reconsider that relationship or friendship. Yes, as adults, we all have things going on in our lives. However, people make time for the relationships that they value. They check on the people who matter to them. They don't only care for them when they need something.

<u>Note to self:</u>
Just because it's not cheating doesn't mean it's not disrespectful as fuck to the relationship.
9:12 PM.

Besides having sexual relations with another person, there are still many other things that you don't do out of respect to your partner and your relationship. Even cheating, itself, doesn't begin with the sexual act itself. It begins with hidden conversations, flirting with intent, and other things of that nature.

<u>Note to self:</u>
It's always what I deserve over who I want.
6:36 AM.

Please stop letting your lust or who you like have priority over how you deserve to be treated. Yes, you should be attracted to your partner, but being with someone should never cause you to abandon your self worth. Finding someone you're attracted to isn't the hard part. The trick is finding someone who not only shares that attraction, but also values you and treats you with respect.

<u>Note to self:</u>
Fuck "going with the flow". What the fuck do you want from me? Because 9 times out of 10, they know. 3:12 PM.

Stop letting people feed you that line about "going with the flow". That is a phrase often used by men who have no intent on being serious. And if something serious is what you are looking for, then take that as a sign that maybe, you should consider not 'wasting' your time with that person.

<u>Note to self:</u>
Don't forget to update your block list, today.
9:29 AM.

Everyone doesn't deserve access to you. Often, you should evaluate your relationships, friendships, and "situationships", and decide what individuals deserve a role in your life, and the ones who are just there taking up space or bringing in negative energy.

<u>Note to self:</u>
Time reveals all fuck boys.
4:56 AM.

People can pretend for a while. But eventually, time will reveal a person's true self and intent. I pray you choose someone who turns out to be everything they show you in the beginning.

<u>Note to self:</u>
Practice letting go and letting God. Start now. 6:16 PM.

<u>Note to self:</u>
Instead of spending the time that you are single just waiting, spend it growing into everything you want to be.
2:11 AM.

Too many single people spend their time waiting or searching for a relationship when they should spend it growing chasing every dream and potential they have. Use that time to find yourself. Use that time to be selfish. Use that time to live and explore. Everything does not have to revolve around a man, or woman. Make everything revolve around you and becoming the best version of yourself.

<u>Note to self:</u>
Fall back in love with yourself. I mean, really really love yourself...
the way you want somebody else to. Set the tone!
4:38 PM.

Don't let that heartbreak discourage you. Don't let it make you forget all that you are and have to offer. Don't let someone who was incapable of seeing how amazing you are cause you to doubt yourself. Don't let yourself down after someone else did.

<u>Note to self:</u>
"Growth" is being able to say "no" to him when your body wants you to say "yes". Because you realize that the B.S that will come with it is simply not worth it. 4:22 AM.

A woman who isn't a slave to her sexual desires is a dangerous woman. This type of self-discipline, especially with someone you have become comfortable with, is hard but so necessary when trying to move on.

<u>Note to self:</u>
Learn to be patient with love. Don't let "relationship goals" rush you.
8:37 AM.

Everyone is trying to be a "cute couple". I'm trying to be a couple that's in a healthy ass loving relationship. That "cute" part doesn't take much. Some people are in toxic, miserable ass relationships and still making it look cute for social media. I'll pass on that.

<u>Note to self:</u>
Unlearn that notion that love is pain.
8:22 PM.

Love is not pain. Love is not disrespect. Love is not uncertainty. Your love, your relationship should not be a constant battlefield. On the contrary, it should be your place of refuge from everything else.

Note to self:
The reality is that on the quest to finding real love, you're probably going to get disappointed a few times. But in the end, when it happens, it'll be worth it. 6:13 AM.

Falling in love has it's risks. Because it's one of those things that you just don't know if you're falling for the right one, until you know. But you can't get to that beautiful fairytale ending that we all desire unless you take those risks; unless you get back up after being let down, broken, and disappointed. The fight for love, real love, is always worth it.

<u>Note to self:</u>
Stop talking yourself out of leaving a man who doesn't talk himself out of cheating on you.
8:22 AM.

Before you make excuses for him, ask yourself why. Ask yourself if it's worth it. Ask yourself why what is stopping you from leaving didn't stop him from continuously disrespecting you. Ask yourself what you expect to change.

<u>Note to self:</u>
His effort will speak loud.
7:38 PM.

As the saying goes "actions speak louder than words". Learn to stop ignoring what someone shows you because of what you hope for, or want with that person. The way they feel about you shows in their actions. Even their intentions with you will show in their actions even if they don't make it clear with words. Pay attention.

<u>Note to self:</u>
You deserve someone who looks at you and is proud that you are theirs and they are yours.
8:16 AM.

<u>Note to self:</u>
You're allowed to say "no" without an explanation.
9:12 PM.

You don't owe everyone an explanation. "No" is a complete sentence. You have the right to dismiss whatever you deem is not for you, and be unapologetic about it. Your space is yours to control. Maintaining your peace doesn't start with removing toxic people, it starts with avoiding them in the first place.

<u>Note to self:</u>
Make sure the next man you choose can elevate you mentally.
4:34 AM.

A man should be able to teach his woman things; and do so without making her feel like she is less than. That's a real man.

<u>Note to self:</u>
Be out of reach to anything that threatens your peace. 6:54 PM.

<u>Note to self:</u>
**Stop dealing with men who say shit like "I can't control her texting me" and get you a "Babe, I blocked her on everything, and she'll never be an issue again" kind of man.
7:55 PM.**

Too many men like making excuses in situations like this, because in reality, they either don't want to accept that they are complicit in the REOCCURING advances from the particular women who seem to not respect boundaries, or they don't want these activities to stop. Either way, that is a bad sign. A man who values you should care about the discomfort these kind of situations cause, and not even want to be complicit in anything that could threaten the relationship.

<u>Note to self:</u>
The moment you hesitate, I lose interest.
11:46 PM.

I don't want anyone who hesitates to choose me. I don't want anyone who I have to convince to choose me. I don't have time to prove my worth to anyone, period!

<u>Note to self:</u>
Men who don't qualify are typically the ones that will say you are asking for too much. Stay away from them. 7:45 PM.

You aren't asking for too much. You are asking for what you believe you deserve. Your value is in your hands, and no one else's. Those who cannot offer that should not ask you to cheapen yourself for their convenience; they should look somewhere else for someone who is asking for what they are offering.

<u>Note to self:</u>
Stop allowing your peace to be interrupted by men who are still deciding if they want you.
5:28 PM.

You don't need to create time for anyone who is unsure. They should make up their mind before they even approach you and interrupt your life. It is selfish of a man to come into a woman's life, convince her to make time, and invest energy, just to string her along while he decides if he truly wants her.

<u>Note to self:</u>
Letting a man put you through hell is not the path to real love; it's the path to pain, resentment, and continuous abuse.
4:36 AM.

<u>Note to self:</u>
Stop keeping people around because of how long you've known them. All toxic people must go. Learn to love people from afar.
9:04 AM.

Let me be the one to tell you that having history with someone doesn't mean a damn thing. You could have dated someone for 5 years and they still don't have your best interest at heart. Too many have the mentality of "The devil you know is better than the devil you don't". The problem with that mentality is that it assumes that everyone else you meet will be no good. That's false. Good men exist. There is better out there. Wait for it.

<u>Note to self:</u>
All break-ups aren't followed by pain. Some are followed by peace.
8:18 AM.

So often we look at break-ups as a bad thing. Truth is, sometimes, a break-up could be the blessing that you have been praying for. Sometimes, a break-up can liberate you. Sometimes, the person you are trying to be happy with, is the person keeping you from being happy.

Note to self:

At any point, you have the right to say "enough is enough". Stop waiting till you are drained completely to get out of an unhealthy situation.
7:11 PM.

Start taking more control and responsibility for how much time you choose to invest in things that are negatively impacting your life. Do not allow yourself to get comfortable with disrespect or any kind of toxic situation.

Note to self:
Your feelings are valid. You're not tripping, overreacting, or doing too much. Don't let anyone take away your right to feel, and express those feelings. 9:56 PM.

<u>Note to self:</u>
Not every woman is replaceable.
1:12 PM.

Chemistry, and loyalty are hard to come by in this generation. A woman who will stick by you had have your best interest at heart doesn't come by often. We have to learn to stop trading a good thing for a good time.

<u>Note to self:</u>
The moment you feel like he is not the one, let him go. 12:55 PM.

The more time you waste holding on to a man you know is not the one for you, the more time you are keeping yourself away from the one who is. Unless you are just dating for fun, you should not be holding on to anyone beyond the point of realizing they aren't the one for you.

<u>Note to self:</u>
If he's not going to respect you, then liking you means nothing.
9:44 PM.

I don't care who likes you, or how much he claims he does; does he respect you? Does he value you? Those are the things that matter. Those are the things that will separate him from others, and those are the people you should choose to invest your time in.

<u>Note to self:</u>
Sometimes, you just have to be like "damn, I got played", and let that shit go.
6:31 AM.

It happens to the best of us. We have to learn to stop dwelling on our failed attempts, and move on. Yes, you had your time wasted. Yes, he lied to you. Yes, you thought it could have been something. It wasn't. You can't change what happened. You can only use what it taught you to try to be more careful, moving forward.

Note to self:
Don't let him keep making decisions and calling them mistakes.
5:42 AM.

The first time may have been a mistake. Even the second time could have been a mistake. But if he keeps doing the same thing over and over, then it is a decision. He either doesn't want to change it, or simply isn't trying to. Stop sweeping it under the rug and sending the message that you are willing to continue to tolerate it if you're not.

<u>Note to self:</u>
He has to respect you even when he is upset.
3:19 PM.

This is what really separates the boys from the men, and speaks so much to someone's character. When, no matter how upset they are at you, or what temporary disagreement you have with them, they don't disrespect you to your face, or behind your back.

<u>Note to self:</u>
I know you planned a whole future with him in your head, and it hurts to accept this, but Sweetheart, he's not the one.
4:29 AM.

One of the toughest things to do is accept that everything you imagined a person will be to you is not going to happen. But it's so necessary in beginning your healing process. As long as you continue to hold on to that idea, it'll be impossible for you to heal.

<u>Note to self:</u>
The problem is you keep choosing men who keep choosing themselves. That shit won't work.
6:14 PM.

If you're choosing him, and he is also choosing himself, then who is choosing you? Stop being all about someone who is also all about themselves. You matter in all of this. You deserve love, and attention as well. You can't just be pouring into someone and getting nothing in return.

<u>Note to self:</u>
Learn to fall in love with the way he loves you.
8:18 AM.

The key is to fall in love with more than just what meets the eye. Fall in love with the way he loves you, treats you, respects you. Fall in love with even the way he looks at you. That's the kind of love that lasts beyond the "honeymoon phase".

<u>Note to self:</u>
I have peace. What I need is loyalty, great sex, amazing conversations, and an effortless vibe.
12:16 PM.

<u>Note to self:</u>
You deserve to feel wanted by the person you chose. 1:19 AM.

It's not about messaging her every 2 seconds. It's about making her feel wanted. Inquiring about her day. Letting her know she's on your mind, and not giving her so much room to wonder. Make her feel important. It's not that complicated, honestly.

__Note to self:__
Too many cheating men are looking for loyal women. 11:59 PM.

Don't let yourself be damaged by a man who never deserved you, in the first place. Watch out for men who want someone that they can come home to after a long day of cheating.

<u>Note to self:</u>
Moving on is all the revenge you need.
4:34 PM.

Just be happy. Move on and focus on you. That's how you win.

<u>Note to self:</u>
Sometimes, them losing you is their karma.
12:12 PM.

When you truly understand how good of a person you are, and the pure intentions you had for someone, you realize that the loss of you is something they will surely come to regret, sooner or later, as they discover that not every woman can be replaced.

<u>Note to self:</u>
Learn the difference between a protective man, and a controlling man.
8:38 AM.

Stop dealing with men who are afraid of you having a life outside of them. You are still an individual. You matter. Your friends matter. Your interests matter. Relationships should not feel like jail or probation. You should have freedom to live, and be trusted to not be out doing anything that may be disrespectful to your relationship

<u>Note to self:</u>
No woman wants a man that brings the "crazy" out of her.
12:47 PM.

Real men understand that the better you treat your woman, the better she treats you. That "peace" that you want her to add to, comes from you treating her right.

<u>Note to self:</u>
Honey, you deserve a man that doesn't mind hurting other women's feelings to protect yours.
7:39 AM.

It should always be you over them. You are priority. You are his teammate. You are his partner. He should never have you continue to be uncomfortable or have legitimate concerns because he is afraid to hurt another woman's feelings with any proposed or necessary resolution to your concerns. Reassuring you takes precedence over outsiders, period!

__Note to self:__
The disrespect hurts worse when you sit back and think about how you would have never done them like that. 7:53 PM.

A lot of times, that's what makes everything hurt more. Feeling like you've been fucking with someone way harder than they fucked with you. Respected them way more than they respected you. Valued them way more than they valued you.

<u>Note to self:</u>
Stop holding on to who he was supposed to be. He lied, Sis.
2:44 PM.

Let go of everything you thought you knew about him that is contradicting everything he is now showing you. People pretend in the beginning. People do their best to be the person they believe you want them to be so that they can get what they want from you.

Note to self:
It's not always just a misunderstanding. Sometimes, they are showing you how they truly feel. Pay close attention. 4:19 PM.

Pay attention to the things people often say and do when they are upset. A lot of times, people use anger or arguments as their excuse to say things that have been on their mind and heart.

<u>Note to self:</u>
Choose someone whose personality excites you. 12:18 PM.

There's something about falling in love with someone's personality that tends to make everything that much more beautiful.

<u>Note to self:</u>
Growth is no longer worrying about what or who your ex is doing.
9:41 PM.

As long as you are still checking up on your ex or watching their moves, you still care. What they are doing with their life should stop being your concern once you decide to move on.

<u>Note to self:</u>
Don't cheat back. Just leave.
4:56 PM.

"Cheating back" doesn't fix the trust that has been broken; it doesn't take away your pain, or that feeling of disappointment; and it definitely does not fix the relationship. It only makes an already toxic environment more toxic.

<u>Note to self:</u>
**Stop stressing over a man who has already started "replacing" you. Go live your best life.
8:39 PM.**

Accept what once was and what no longer is. Let go of people who have already let go of you, and continue on with your life as they have done with theirs.

<u>Note to self:</u>
I'm single because I'm not just out here trying to fill a void. I want something that's going to last.
5:31 PM.

Wait for what you want, and what you deserve. It will find you. There is nothing wrong with you just because you don't care to keep jumping in and out of relationships with people you don't really see a future with.

<u>Note to self:</u>
**Be careful, these men are out here putting women through what they promised to save them from.
7:29 PM.**

A man will claim that he is "different" when he is not. He will convince you that you have been dealing the "wrong kind of men", and end up being the worst kind of man. It's unfortunate, but some men will do or say anything to convince a woman to invest her time into him. Be cautious, and take your time to know people.

<u>Note to self:</u>
**A lot of men don't know what to do with a woman who is unimpressed by what is in his wallet.
4:22 PM.**

<u>Note to self:</u>
Stop holding down men who are only holding back.
10:53 AM.

Make sure you are holding down someone who would do, or does, the same for you. Too often women continue to take care of men who only misuse them, and hinder their growth.

Note to self:

Just because it's taking longer than you would like does not mean it's not happening. One day, you will look up and everything you prayed for will be right in front of you.
4:12 PM.

CPSIA information can be obtained
at www.ICGtesting.com
Printed in the USA
BVHW030743060520
579274BV00004B/255